PASSION!
8 Steps to Find Yours

By Mark J. Lindquist and Jared L. Bye

Look for these books by Mark J. Lindquist and Jared L. Bye coming soon!

- Failure! Don't Be Afraid Of It

- Service! My Way Of Life

- Dreams! The Biggest Thing You Should Own

- They! The Most Influential Group In America

- Action! The Time Is Now

- Priorities! Putting First Things First

- Goals! Knock Them Out of the Park

- Time! Owning It Is Priceless

PASSION! 8 Steps to Find Yours

Step 1: Try a Bunch of Stuff

Step 2: Find Out What You Like

Step 3: Find Your Strength Zone

Step 4: Ask Yourself If You're Passionate About It

Step 5: Don't Stop Until You Find Your Passion

Step 6: Lean-in To Your Passion

Step 7: Take the Money and Run

Step 8: Everything is Possible

Dedicated to:

Aftin, Ainsley and Declan Bye

Gordon and Diane Lindquist

Introduction

Welcome to the next 15 minutes of your life. The next 15 minutes won't be very complicated. We're not splitting the atom or calculating NASA rocket propulsion equations. This is a fun and simple book to help you along your journey in life, no matter what phase of life you happen to be in. If you're a 7th grader, this book can help you get to where you want to be in life. If you're in your 70's and re-inventing yourself as a retiree, this book is for you too.

These are the steps I have followed repeatedly throughout the course of my life and they have led me to the successful and happy life that I live today. I humbly offer them to you with the hope that they will assist you in living a passion-filled life as I do. Be warned, even at Step 1 you are embarking upon the Road Less Traveled. When you get to Step 3, you have done what most won't. By Step 5, you might be the last one standing. Most never make it to Step 6, in fact, only about 11 percent ever will. Step 7 is rare air. Step 8 makes you a PhD. in the game of life.

I wish you well on your journey toward your passion.

Your Friend,
Mark J. Lindquist

Don't believe that the system of success that was handed to you is the best system simply because it was handed to you. What if there was a better way?

—Mark J. Lindquist

Step 1: Try a Bunch of Stuff

This book is the roadmap I have followed on the way to the successful, happy, and passion-filled life I live today. Anyone can follow these steps. It matters not if you are rich or poor, or if you come from a long-line of success or not. It doesn't matter if you live in a big house right now or if you have a studio apartment and eat nothing but peanut butter and jelly sandwiches every day just to stay alive.

Step 1 is easy. Rest assured, we're not going to get too fancy here.

Step 1: Try a bunch of stuff.

Are you a 7th grader? You can do this. In fact, that's when I started intentionally trying a bunch of stuff. You aren't in the 7th grade? No big deal, start now. Not tomorrow, now. After all, this isn't too complicated. You don't need a master plan. You don't need to get ready to get ready. You don't need to wait for the perfect opportunity.

You just need to try.

Try what?

A bunch of stuff.

Now. Go.

Are you back already? Well done. What did you try? Oh, you didn't try anything? Well get outta here. Go try some stuff. I don't care what kind of stuff. Just go try.

Ready... Go!

Ok, now you're back. You tried some stuff.

Did you like it?

No? Go try some other stuff. Now. Not later, now.

Oh good, you're back. Did you try some more stuff?

Did you like it?

Oh goody. You liked the stuff. Now you're ready for Step 2.

"Twenty years from now you will be more disappointed by the things that you didn't do than by the ones you did do. So throw off the bowlines. Sail away from the safe harbor. Catch the trade winds in your sails. Explore. Dream. Discover."

—Mark Twain

Step 2: Find Out What You Like

You liked the stuff? Yay! That's good. I'm super-duper excited for you! You have found something you like. Consider this a win in your life. Don't worry if this is THE THING or YOUR CALLING. It's not that big of a deal. Just be happy you found something you like. There's lots of stuff out there. Some of it you may like, and some of it you may not like. It's fun to do stuff you like. If you want to find more stuff you like, repeat Step 1. Go try a bunch of stuff!

Here's How Life Looks:

Stuff I've Tried

Stuff I Like

Possibilities

Hey! Just do the things you like! Keep a list of these things that you really, really like.

1. _____

2. _____

3. _____

4. _____

5. _____

6. _____

7. _____

8. _____

9. _____

10. _____

If you ever find yourself out of balance, unhappy, sad, depressed, or just plain blah, go back to this list of things you like and start doing them. Begin with number one and keep going until you reach number 10. I bet you will feel much better by the time you get down to the bottom of the list. ☺

Sweet! You've found a bunch of stuff you like! High five! Let's send you on your way to the wonderful world of Step 3.

The two most important days in your life are the day you are born and the day you find out why.

—Mark Twain

Step 3: Find Your Strength Zone

This step is all about finding the things you're good at doing. Not too difficult or complicated here. When you do the things you're good at, you create little victories for your life.

Did you win once? Now see if you can win again. I'm not necessarily talking about winning against an opponent... I think the only win that matters in life is the win you chalk up against your former self.

I have found that my strengths lie in the area of singing, public speaking and entertaining. I didn't start out singing for tens of thousands or speaking for billion-dollar companies; I had to work up to it. I had to build upon my victories over time. I had to discover and continue to work in my strengths.

Find your strengths, my friend. Make this a priority in your life. Odds are good that if you take a look at that list of things that you like, some of those things are probably in your Strength Zone[1].

Let me explain:

Leadership Guru John Maxwell says that everyone has a Strength Zone. As I have applied his Strength Zone principle to my life, I have thought about it like this:

Everyone is on a scale from 1-10 with all the things they do. If you put all your time and energy and effort into one thing, no matter what level you are at, the most you'll probably rise on the scale is by one or two points. For example, if you're a 4 in volleyball, the most you'll probably ever be is a 5 or a 6. Don't worry; if you love volleyball, keep playing! Keep doing it as a hobby, and keep it on the list of things you like.

All I'm saying is that maybe this thing isn't your Strength Zone. However, if you're an 8 in football, then work on football! This is in your Strength Zone! Put all your time and energy and effort into football and maybe you'll become a 9 or 10!

You see, as I understand John Maxwell's teachings on this subject, people won't cross the street for 5's and 6's, but they'll cross oceans and stand in line around the block for 9's and 10's.

Work in your Strength Zone.

You don't have a Strength Zone?

I don't believe you.

If this is how you see yourself, I simply believe that you haven't spent enough time in Step 1, which is Try a Bunch of Stuff.

Here's How I See Your Strengths:

Stuff I've Tried

Stuff I Like

Your Strengths May Be in Here!

Keep trying, my friend! Keep trying a bunch of stuff and you'll find your strengths! If you haven't found them yet, keep searching. There's something out there that is your 7 or 8. Imagine all the possibilities out there for you to try. Many of them are probably outside of your hometown. Many of them may be on another continent. Many of them may be way out of your comfort zone. But rest assured my friend, they are out there.

Your only job is to repeat Steps 1 and 2 until you find your strengths. The mistake most people make is to stop trying new things around the ages of 18 to 20. During this phase of life, people tend to think they have to "figure out what they're going to do with the rest of their life." No way! Don't put that kind of pressure on yourself my friend! You know what the best people say when they're 50 or 60 years old?

They say,

"I'm still trying to figure out what I want to do when I grow up."

AND THEY MEAN IT.

You don't have to find "it" when you're a certain age. You don't have to find it by the time you graduate high school. You don't have to find it by the time you're finished with college. There isn't an expiration date on the dreams you have inside your head and your heart.

Find what you like when you're 30! Great! Find your strengths when you're 40! Super! Just find them, as soon as you can. If you're 70 years old and you feel like you haven't truly identified your strength zone, jump right in to Step 1!

Life's too short to be so serious. Just go try a bunch of stuff. See what you like. Find out where your Strength Zone is.

Then, it's on to the next Step!

---

[1] Maxwell, John C. Leadership Gold: Lessons Learned from a Lifetime of Leading. Nashville: Thomas Nelson, 2008. Print.

We must believe that we are gifted for something, and that this thing, at whatever cost, must be attained.

—Marie Curie

Step 4: Ask Yourself If You're Passionate About It

Did you know that Deloitte[1] performed a recent study on employee passion and they found that 89 percent of American workers don't have passion for what they do?

Phooey! That's garbage! Do you remember the quote I put in the introduction to this handy little book?

> "Don't believe that the system of success that was handed to you is the best system... simply because it was handed to you. What if there was a better way?"
> -Mark J. Lindquist

If the system of success that was handed to you by society is yielding only 11 percent passion, then I suggest we look elsewhere for our cues on how to live our life.

Passion is the key! When you're passionate about what you're doing, it doesn't feel like work. When you're passionate about what you're doing, you'd do it all day long and you'd do it for free. When you're passionate, time flies and you have endless energy to do the things you're passionate about.

I'm 33 years old and I have found my passions in life. I first discovered that singing, public speaking and entertaining were in my strength zone when I was in junior high and high school. I discovered that they were my passions when I was 30 and on a world tour as an entertainer, emcee and vocalist. The lesson to learn here is that I was still asking myself what my passion was when I was 30 years old.

I find that many people either:

A) Never ask themselves what their passion is.

B) Stop asking themselves that question way too early in life.

This is such a shame. In our society, it is as if we feel like we all need to "figure it out" so early in our lives. There is this undeniable pressure for the teenager to figure out what they're doing after high school. The pressure a college student feels to pick a major and a career field they think they'll do well in is only increasing as the job market becomes more and more competitive.

However, after about age 22-24 we simply stop asking ourselves what we want in life. For most people, passion is not a conversation that gets more than a few moments of attention once every couple of years.

Why is this?

It's because life happens. Understandably, we all get caught up in the busy nature of our lives, and before we know it, we wake up and realize that we've spent the last 10 years of our life working for a paycheck and completely forgot about working toward our passion.

What we need to do is hit the "refresh" button in our lives from time to time, and ask ourselves if we're passionate about the things that we spend our time doing.

If the answer is no, then it's time to repeat Steps 1-3.

---

[1] Hagel, John, John Seely Brown, and Tamara Samoylova. Unlocking the Passion of the Explorer: Report 1 of the 2013 Shift Index Series. N.p.: Deloitte UP, 2013. Print.

Definiteness of purpose is the starting point of all achievement.

—W. Clement Stone

Step 5: Don't Stop Until You Find Your Passion

I Look at the Process of Finding Your Passion Like this:

100 Things You Can Do in Life

Passions = #54, #70, and #83

Let's say that there are 100 things you can do in life. There are obviously many, many more, but for the sake of this exercise, let's say there are 100.

I believe everyone has a passion or multiple passions. As you search for this passion, everyone starts at #1, as you see in this picture. You try one thing and then we move on to the next, just like in Step 1 - Try a Bunch of Stuff.

A lot of people stop trying a bunch of stuff before they find their strengths. Most people stop trying a bunch of stuff before they find their passion(s). In this example (see picture), let's say that this person's passions are #54, #70 and #83. But look at what happened – This person stopped trying stuff at #35.

Maybe this person was 23 years old. Maybe they were 47 years old when they stopped at #35 on the list. Maybe they got busy with life, like paying a mortgage, having a big girl/boy job. Maybe they got married and started a family and forgot about trying new stuff, and they forgot about finding their strengths and passions. All those things are great and a wonderful part of life! But how come they stopped at #35? Did the velocity of life take over? Did they forget one of the basic principles of a happy and successful life, which is to find your passion?

My point is, this person stopped before they found their passion. They stopped trying a bunch of stuff. If they had just kept with it for a little while longer, they would have found their first passion, which was waiting for them at #54. If they had really kept with it then they would have come across #70, which was their second passion… and #83 and so on and so forth.

When I was in high school, and they had me take an aptitude test that was supposed to tell me "What I was supposed to be when I grew up," I didn't see anything on the list that I was fired up about. I saw things like doctor, lawyer, engineer, computer technician, pharmacist, farmer, and teacher. Now, there's absolutely nothing wrong with those occupations, none whatsoever. But I didn't see my passion or even my strengths on that list.

Nobody ever told me that I could be a production assistant on the set of a blockbuster Hollywood movie like "Battleship." I never was a production assistant, but I didn't learn that this was even a real thing until I acted in the movie when I was 29 years old.

Nobody ever told me that I could be an audio technician for a world touring entertainment group. I never was, but I didn't even know that this job existed until I saw my good friend Mike work as an audio technician on our world tour in 2011.

Nobody ever told me that I could be a wild land firefighter for the National Park Service and jump out of airplanes and helicopters like my good buddy Gifford Wong. I never jumped out of planes and helicopters, but I sure did fight wild land fires in the Shenandoah Valley and the Great Smoky Mountains. Nobody ever told me I could do those things. They simply weren't on the list.

Refer back to that picture in Step 2. The larger portion of the pie contains the possibilities that exist in the world. Who knows what you'll like, what you're good at, and ultimately what your passions are until you try enough things to have a sample large enough to call it "data."

My success and the happy and passionate life I live today is due to the fact that as I started at #1 and kept trying new stuff. Through life's journey, I didn't stop until I found my passion. At age 30 I was still searching. I didn't stop. I didn't settle. I kept progressing through Steps 1-4 over and over and over again until I found my passions.

On July 5th, 2014 I turned 33 years old. On that exact day I was engaged in one of my passions at approximately 1:10 p.m. Central Standard Time. The Minnesota Twins invited me to sing our National Anthem for their Saturday home game against the New York

Yankees on July 5th. I stood 10 feet from Derek Jeter and saw myself on the Jumbotron as we honored our nation. It was the largest audience I have performed for in my career (over 36,000 at Target Field in Minneapolis) and one of the most significant days of my life thus far. Some of the umpires even told me it was the best anthem they had ever heard. Considering that those umpires have probably heard thousands of National Anthem renditions throughout their careers, I consider that a win!

It was such a thrill to sing for one of the biggest games of the season and stand on the same field where they would play the 2014 All-Star Game just a few weeks later. I wouldn't have had this privilege at age 33 if I had stopped searching for my passion earlier in life.

Passion. Find yours.

If you haven't found it, repeat Steps 1-4 with happiness in your heart and a smile on your face! This process is the most exciting, exhilarating and energetic process there ever could be – because at the end of the journey, you find your PASSION!

Are there going to be bumps along the road as you try a bunch of stuff, find what you like, find your strength zone and then your passions? Sure! But you're going to live through those years of your life anyway, so you might as well find your strengths and passions as soon as possible! Then, you can live the rest of your years as the best, most authentic, passionate version of you! Yay!

I get to live the next 70 years of my life as the passionate Mark J. Lindquist. I get to offer the passionate and authentic me to the world for the remainder of my life. This is why I look toward the future with extreme excitement and zeal for what is to come.

This is what I want for you, my friend. Just repeat Steps 1-4. See you along the journey – I'm excited for you!

Your work is going to fill a large part of your life, and the only way to be truly satisfied is to do what you believe is great work. And the only way to do great work is to love what you do. If you haven't found it yet, keep looking. Don't settle.

—Steve Jobs

Step 5 is such an important step! This, above all is the step I hope you follow, my friend! Pretty please? Pretty please with a super-duper cherry on top? Just don't stop. Don't settle. For goodness sake, don't settle.

My friends, I always knew what I wanted to be when I grew up. No, it's not what you're thinking. I wanted to be the grandpa on the front porch with all the neighborhood kids gathered around my rocking chair. When the kiddos asked me about my life, I never wanted to be the guy who looked back at life and said, "I wish I would have." I always wanted to be the guy who looked down at that group of young people and had hundreds of stories about **the times that I'm glad I did**. That's the life I want to live. I want to be able to tell the story to the next generation and beyond that I went out and gave this life my all – that I squeezed the most out of my 100+ years on this earth and left nothing on the table. This is the type of life I wish for you. This is the type of life you can have if you don't stop until you find your passion.

Be that grandpa on the front porch who tells tales of adventure. Be the role model for other young people and live a life that leads them to say, "When I grow up I want to be just like him!" Be that guy.

If you're just starting out in life, I want to encourage you. Don't let the world tell you that you have to live a certain life. Don't let the world tell you that you have to be an XYZ by age 22. Don't let the world tell you that you are a failure if you don't do A, B and C. What if you want to do D, E, and F? Or for goodness sake, what if you want to do F, E, and then D? Write your own story my friend. Blaze your own trail. This is what I've done for the past 15 years and now I live the most exciting, happy, successful, passion-filled life that I can imagine. That's what I'm doing. I'm living the life I have imagined. All because I didn't stop. The life I live today is due to the fact that I followed these steps and was constantly in pursuit of my passions.

I finally found my passions. I wish this for you. Because once you've found your passions, then it is as if life opens up the fast lane for you. When you find what some call "your authentic self" which is the version of you that is totally aligned with the person you are "supposed to be," then you are winning. Once you've found your passion, then it doesn't feel like work. Every day is exciting. Literally. Every day. Of course, it's not all sunshine and lollipops just because you've stuck with these steps long enough to find your passion. There will be hard days too. Life will throw you a curveball or two, just like everyone else has to deal with. However, I would rather live my life as a passionate person, on fire for how I spend my time and how I impact the world around me... rather than be a broke down and busted, bored, frustrated, stuck version of myself.

People will tell you to give it up. People will tell you that you're crazy. People will pass all kinds of judgments on you because you're coloring outside the lines. Forget them. It's not their life. It's your life. Your passions. Your impact on the world. This is your time. This is your chance. Don't stop until you've found your passions, it is the most worthwhile journey you can ever embark upon.

I'm passionate. I'm passionate about who I am. I'm passionate about what I do. I'm passionate about how I make my impact in the world. I'm passionate simply because I refused to stop until I found my passions.

Don't stop. Keep charging. You can do it. It's worth it.

> *It is not the critic who counts; not the man who points out how the strong man stumbles, or where the doer of deeds could have done them better. The credit belongs to the man who is actually in the arena, whose face is marred by dust and sweat and blood; who strives valiantly; who errs, who comes short again and again, because there is no effort without error and shortcoming; but who does actually strive to do the deeds; who knows great enthusiasms, the great devotions; who spends himself in a worthy cause; who at the best knows in the end the triumph of high achievement, and who at the worst, if he fails, at least fails while daring greatly, so that his place shall never be with those cold and timid souls who neither know victory nor defeat.*

Teddy Roosevelt
The Man in the Arena, April 23, 1910

Step 6: Lean-in To Your Passion

Whew! You've made it through Steps 1-5! Winner! Now you're on to Step 6 - the realm where few can say they have walked. If only 11 percent of people find their passion, even fewer truly "lean-in" to their passion. So now, the only thing left to do is... Do it all the time! Do as much of it as possible! Do it now! Do it tomorrow! Do it for the rest of your life!

Do you think Edison was passionate? Einstein? Martin Luther King Jr.? Oprah? Bill Gates? Mother Teresa? Michelangelo? Beethoven? Sure they were! And once they found their passion, they leaned-in to it. This is the reason why we know their names today.

Can you be one of these greats? Absolutely! You can make it on lists like these. You can be one of the greats throughout history if that's your goal! You have a chance to do it if you lean-in to your passion. However, your chances of being a world-changer and a difference maker drastically decrease if you aren't willing to do what is necessary to find your passion. Similarly, if you choose not to lean-in to your passion once you have found it, odds are good you'll never be mentioned in history books either. So find that passion and lean-in! Let's change the world!

So my friends, let's choose passion! Let's go for it! What have we got to lose? If you live your life like everyone else does, chances are, you'll end up as a person without passion for what you do... and who wants to be like that? Not me! We have a choice!

What we have to do is try a bunch of stuff. Then we have to find out what we like. After that, we find out what we're good at and discover where our strengths are. If we're fortunate, then we align our strengths with passion for that thing. We are the type of people who don't stop until we find our passion. Then, our job is to lean-in to that passion, do it as often as possible and live a life designed around that passion.

Now you're really cooking!! You're on your way to living a passion-filled life!!!

On to the next Step!!!

If one advances confidently in the direction of his dreams, and endeavors to live the life which he has imagined, he will meet with success unexpected in common hours.

—Henry David Thoreau

Step 7: Take the Money and Run

My good friend and Motivational Speaker Bill Johnson is credited with this phrase as it relates to passion: "Take the money and run!"

If you're persistent enough to find your passion, that's AWESOME! If you're really, really fortunate and you can find someone to pay you for the thing that you're passionate about - TAKE THE MONEY AND RUN. You've now hit the jackpot.

Now, some people say things like, "I don't want to do it for a living, because I might get burned out on it."

It is my opinion that if someone is burned out on doing the thing they thought was their passion, than one of two things is happening:

    1) You may not have found your true passion.

You are not likely to burn out on your true passion. When you have found your true passion, your actions reflect your "authentic self," or the "you" that you are meant to be. You don't get burned out when you are being your authentic self because it is the best possible version of you – The authentic you. What may be happening when you feel burned out is that you actually just found something that you liked and was in your Strength Zone. It may not have been the passion I'm talking about. Go back and repeat Steps 1-6. You'll find it!

> 2) You're probably not burned out on the thing for which you're passionate; there are probably other factors that are burning you out.

It is more likely that the details and responsibilities that come along with pursuing your passion are the burnout factors we should blame, not the passion itself. These factors can include: running your own business, negotiating contracts, being away from your family, being on the road, stress due to unsteady paychecks, etc. Maybe all these things are not in your Strength Zone, so the necessity of spending your time doing these things makes you feel burned out.

Allow me to give a simple example:

Jenny loves flowers. She loves creating fancy arrangements and is delighted by the idea that her work makes someone's day. However, Jenny is a solo entrepreneur and flower shop owner who has pursued her passion for flowers on her own with no staff. Although Jenny is a master florist and has a creative nature that makes her shop one of the most popular in town, she feels burned out after a couple of years. She starts to question whether this path is correct, and whether it is worth tainting her one true love, which is creating beautiful floral arrangements. She decides to sell the floral shop with the rationale that she doesn't want to ruin her lifelong passion for flowers by doing it for a living.

Did Jenny get burned out on her passion for flowers? No. She loved that part of her gig. She could create floral arrangements all day long, and she'd probably do it for free if she could. What she got burned out on were the other details of running a business that weren't in her Strength Zone. You see, creating floral arrangements that make an impact on people's lives is in her Strength Zone. However, bookkeeping, advertising, purchase orders, taxes, negotiations, supply chains and building maintenance are not in her Strength Zone.

When we talk about passion burnout, typically there are other factors that are creating the drain and feeling of burnout. We need to recognize that it is not our passion that is wavering; it is our inability to work outside our Strength Zone in the other duties that give us that feeling of burnout.

If you do start to experience passion burn out, count yourself lucky that you ever found your passion in the first place! Back off a bit and re-engage with your passion as time goes on. After all, you have to remember that only 11 percent of people end up engaging in their passion anyway, so you're still the winner! And remember, you can have multiple passions, as I do. We're all human beings with an almost infinite number of varying interests, hobbies, skills, viewpoints, thoughts and passions.

If you're fortunate enough to find someone to pay you for the thing that you're passionate about, yes, take the money and run. Don't feel guilty about it. Take it. Be proud of it. Consider this a win.

Now I'm not suggesting you quit your full-time job the moment the first check comes in. We all need a better business plan than that if we're going to truly succeed in a passion-filled life. However, count yourself lucky if you are able to earn money – or even make a decent living – by doing something for which you are passionate. I certainly feel fortunate for this component of my life, and I wish the same success for you.

*If you do what you love you'll
never work a day in your life.*

—Marc Anthony

Step 8: Everything Is Possible

My success in life comes down to the very first mindset that is taught in Scott Shickler and Jeff Waller's book, "The 7 Mindsets." I believe Everything Is Possible. Not just some things. Everything. Not just every other thing. Not just the things that happen on the third Tuesday of the month after the lunar eclipse. Everything Is Possible. Everything.

This mindset allows me to dream big and set awesome goals. Some of them I achieve and some of them still reside in my head and in my heart. But at the center of my world is the belief that truly everything is possible. It is how I live my life. It is my mantra. It is how I make decisions in my life. It is what I know to be true.

What if you don't think that Everything Is Possible? What if you don't have that ability, perspective, mindset, or way about you? Well, I believe that what you need to do is progress through Steps 1-7 and prove to yourself that Everything Is Possible. You need to start trying a bunch of stuff, find what you like and then find your Strength Zone. When you do things you are good at, then you will begin to collect little victories throughout your life. These victories, large and small, will serve as proof that you can do anything – they will serve as proof that what you were told in kindergarten is actually true: Everything Is Possible.

You can be, do and have whatever you want. Everything Is Possible, my friend. I ask you this question: Have you done something in your life that upon the successful completion you proved to yourself that you can do anything? If not, what can you choose to do this year that will serve as proof that you can do anything? Identify that thing and start trying. Start with the little things and build to the bigger things. This is not to say that you won't experience any setbacks or failure, those are things that can happen in life too. However, I challenge you to begin a relentless journey to prove to yourself that Everything IS Possible and that you CAN do anything. Start small. Build bigger. This process may even take you many years. But the reward on the other side is nothing shy of magic.

When you truly believe that Everything Is Possible, then the entire world opens up to you. As for me, I have set some pretty cool goals and I have been hitting many of them. When I first started out in Steps 1-3 I would audition for 10 things and maybe I would get one or two gigs. Over the years, I have honed my craft, rehearsed relentlessly, and have been dedicated to my strengths and my passions. Now my success ratio has increased drastically. These days, I may audition for 10 things and maybe I get 7 or 8 gigs. I think that this is the result of repeatedly progressing through Steps 1-6.

I believe Everything is Possible. Everything.

One day, I am going to sing the National Anthem at the Super Bowl. Do I know how that is going to happen? No. But I believe it is possible. By the end of 2014 I will have performed live for over a million people throughout my career... so absolutely I believe this is possible. So far, I have soloed the National Anthem at RFK Stadium; for the Minnesota Twins; in front of the New York Yankees; for country artists Jarrod Niemann and The Band Perry; for the Los Angeles Dodgers; and I have landed the full-time National Anthem gig with one of the top NCAA Men's Hockey programs in the nation, the University of North Dakota. These victories I have collected over years of working through Steps 1-6 have convinced me that the dream of singing at the Super Bowl is indeed possible. Think about how I progressed through the 8 Steps with this one simple passion, the National Anthem.

Step 1: First, I tried a bunch of stuff – I sang every song I could get my hands on.

Step 2: I found out that of all the songs there were to perform, I liked The Star-Spangled Banner the most.

Step 3: After a few performances and repeated rehearsal, I discovered that performing The Star-Spangled Banner was in my Strength Zone. People would often tell me they appreciated that I sang the song the "right" way, without all the embellishments and runs. Audience members would often tell me it was one of the best renditions they had ever heard.

Step 4: As I got older, I asked myself if I was passionate about it. Remember one of the indicators of passion: Would you do it for free? I sure would, and I did. Nobody ever paid me for the hundreds of Anthem performances I delivered while I was in the United States Military. I did it because I was passionate about singing the song and delivering it the way I believe it should be performed.

Step 5: I started singing when I was a freshman in high school, but I didn't start singing the National Anthem until I was a junior in high school. At that point in my life, I don't know if I knew that performing the National Anthem was a passion of mine – I just knew I liked it and it was a strength. Years later, when I was singing the Anthem for Rihanna, Liam Neeson, and the cast and crew of Universal Studios "Battleship," I discovered that this was a passion of mine. I was 29 years old, and still searching for my passions.

Step 6: I've been leaning-in to my passion as I have auditioned for Anthem gigs at some of the largest events in the nation, and luckily, I have been given quite a few.

Step 7: Anthem gigs traditionally don't pay, but when they do – I take the money and run. One day, it is my dream to be known throughout the country as the premiere National Anthem singer in the United States. If you have a sold-out event and you need an Afghanistan War Veteran to deliver a crowd pleasing and rousing National Anthem – you call me. Once we reach that level, we'll abide by that old adage: "If you're good at something, don't do it for free."

Step 8: With this Step, I have applied the concept of Everything Is Possible to my specific passion of National Anthem singing. Everything Is Possible in my world, including singing on the big-gest stage on the planet: The Super Bowl. You see, most people don't find their passion. Amongst those that do, most people don't stretch themselves within that passion to dream their best dreams and apply the Everything Is Possible mindset to it. If you do, then Super Bowl-type dreams can be a part of your life. This is what I wish for you.

My friends, if you find your passion, lean-in to that passion and then apply the Everything Is Possible mindset to your passion – you have unlocked a combination that an extremely small percentage of people will ever experience. If the steps in this book help you to find your passion, then the last step is to believe Everything Is Possible. That is what Edison did and why he made such progress with the light bulb. The Wright Brothers found their passion, and they believed Everything Is Possible, even when the rest of the world may have thought they were crazy.

Do you see where we're going here? I believe that the basis for great achievement and meaning in your life may start with this book. Passion. Passion is what matters, my friend. If you can find your passion, then you're ahead of 89 percent of the American population. If you can truly embrace the idea that you can do anything and that Everything Is Possible, then you have a real chance at being mentioned in history books and on lists of the greatest who ever lived.

To give your **passionate** *self to the world is the greatest gift you can give the world.*

—Mark J. Lindquist

Afterword

After 15 years of relentless searching, I have found my strengths, I discovered that I am passionate about those strengths, I lean-in to my passion and today I believe Everything is Possible. I have followed these 8 Steps to Find Your Passion, and now I am equipped to conquer the world. What world? Whatever world I choose to conquer.

Since I believe Everything is Possible, one day I am going to write a best-selling book. One day, I am going to have a live show on the Vegas Strip. One day, I'll be a game show host. One day, I'll replace Michael Buffer as the ring announcer at fights and at the MGM Grand. One day, I will perform my Sinatra-Style variety show to stadiums full of tens of thousands of people. One day, people will know my name like they do Harry Connick Jr., Michael Buble, Tony Bennett and Frank Sinatra. One day, I will sing our National Anthem at every major sporting event in the country. One day, I will be in more movies and back on TV. One day, I will be as well-known as Tony Robbins on the motivational speaking circuit. One day, I will be an entrepreneur with hundreds of successful businesses like Richard Branson. One day, I will have a foundation like the Bill and Melinda Gates Foundation and make an impact in the lives of people around the globe with our philanthropic efforts. One day, I'll have a real estate empire like Donald Trump. One day, I will travel to every country on earth.

Passion is the fuel that drives your big dreams. Everything is Possible. Everything.

I want this for you. Follow these 8 Steps to Find Your Passion. It is my playbook. It is my hard-work, heartache, blood, sweat and tears that have brought me to these 8 Steps. I have achieved a little in my life, but I have so much more ahead of me. I want you to live the same type of passion filled life that I do. It is the only way to live. I am 33 years old at the time of this writing and I am so darn excited about what is ahead for me in the next 70+ years that I can barely contain my enthusiasm for life. I am the happiest person I know. I believe I am that way because of the steps I have followed and the passions I have discovered.

Come along with me on this journey toward your passionate life.

All it takes is a single step.

Step 1: Try a Bunch of Stuff

Step 2: Find Out What You Like

Step 3: Find Your Strength Zone

Step 4: Ask Yourself If You're Passionate About It

Step 5: Don't Stop Until You Find Your Passion

Step 6: Lean-in To Your Passion

Step 7: Take the Money and Run

Step 8: Everything is Possible

Making Our Impact on the World

I give my passionate self to the world as often as I possibly can. As a motivational speaker, entertainer, and entrepreneur I seek to make my impact on the world in many ways. Primarily, I deliver keynote speeches at conferences and conventions, for corporate meetings and employee gatherings. I also deliver school assemblies at middle and high schools and I speak at youth conferences, colleges and Young Professionals Networks. Another one of my passions is found in the realm of volunteerism; for that reason I also speak for non-profit groups, civic organizations and service clubs.

My business manager, long-time best friend, and like-minded champion of passion, Mr. Jared L. Bye is the one who makes all of this happen. He is truly the "brains behind our operation" and makes it possible for our companies to make the impact that we do. We speak to people as young as 5th graders all the way up to the CEO's and business leaders at billion dollar companies. When we are out on the road and on stage, you'll find us delivering keynotes on three different topics:

Passion. Leadership. Service.

At Breath Is Limited Motivational Speaking and Entertainment, LLC we are in the business of "Advancing Ideas… Igniting Passion." Our goal is to lead as many people as possible toward the discovery of their passions. We seek to inspire, entertain, and lead others toward their passionate self.

Here is our full topic list as of August of 2014:

Also found at www.BreathIsLimited.com

Passion! 8 Steps to Find Yours
Based on our book, "PASSION! 8 Steps to Find Yours," Mark will deliver a talk packed with fun and overflowing with excitement about how to live a life filled with passion. This presentation is a hit with students and adults alike! Suitable for Corporate Audiences and School Assemblies.

Military Leadership Lessons for Corporate America
Drawing from his experiences leading an elite military unit throughout 22 countries and 39 states, Mark will deliver a captivating presentation about military culture and traditions that influence leadership decisions inside one of the most revered institutions in our nation. Suitable for Corporate Audiences and Youth Leadership.

Opportunity Ahead

Mark has been more places and has experienced more incredible things than most have ever dreamed of. Allow this world-touring entertainer, Hollywood actor, nationally recognized singer, author and motivational speaker to show you to the opportunities that exist in your life. This is a show-stopping talk about finding your passion and seizing opportunities meant for you. Suitable for Corporate Audiences and School Assemblies.

9/11/2001: Lessons From Ground Zero

Mark was an American Red Cross Emergency Responder at the Pentagon in the days following 9/11. He delivers a riveting talk about his experiences supporting the true heroes that emerged from this national tragedy. Audiences will leave with a common language and the ability to recall "the best person they have ever been." Suitable for Corporate Audiences, School Assemblies and Classroom Presentations.

Service, My Way of Life
Mark has been living a life dedicated to service and volunteerism for the past 18 years. He has served in the U.S. Military and is an Afghanistan War Veteran; he has served in Clinton's AmeriCorps and has his picture in the Presidential Library in Little Rock, Arkansas; he has built houses for Habitat for Humanity as well as playgrounds for inner-city youth in almost every major city in the nation. Mark will inspire you with his tales of service all over the globe and leave your audiences ready to go out and change the world. Suitable for Civic Organizations, Youth Groups, School Assemblies and Corporate Community Involvement departments.

The 7 Mindsets to Live Your Ultimate Life
Want to know how the most successful and happy people got to where they are? The 7 Mindsets to Live Your Ultimate Life (Written by Scott Shickler and Jeff Waller) are the result of a multi-year, multi-million dollar research project that uncovered the key component of a person's success and happiness: Their Mindset. Mark will teach you how to live what we call, "Your Ultimate Life." Suitable for Corporate Audiences, School Assemblies, Full and Half-Day Training for Youth and Adults.

Own the Stage

Mark has performed live for over 750,000 people throughout his career for audiences around the globe. He has performed for staffers at the White House, at NATO Headquarters in Europe, for NFL players, Major League Baseball, the NCAA and the NHL. Mark will pass on his vast experience, rehearsal tips, techniques, strategies to own the crowd, and presentation knowledge that will make you look like a pro. Suitable for anyone wishing to improve their stage presence, skills and abilities.

Breath Is Limited Conference Services
The compliment we most often receive is, "Mark was the best hour of our conference!" Allow us to make your entire event, "The best conference in decades."

We offer:
- Keynotes
- Breakout Sessions
- Half-Day Trainings
- World-Class Emceeing
- Live Sinatra-Style Entertainment (Solo, 60-90 Minute Set)
- Live Sinatra-Style Entertainment (Live 9 Piece Band, 60-90 Minute Set)

Few speakers can make an impact at your upcoming conference in the many ways Mark J. Lindquist can.

Find us at www.BreathIsLimited.com!!

About the Co-Author Mark J. Lindquist

Mark J. Lindquist is a nationally recognized motivational speaker and world-touring entertainer who has performed live for over 750,000 people in 22 countries and 44 states throughout his career. As an actor, he has appeared in ABC's LOST, CBS' Hawaii Five-O and the Universal Studios movie "Battleship." He has performed for Grammy winning artists, Academy Award nominated actors, foreign dignitaries around the world as well as staffers at the White House. Mark has been featured on CNN.com, C-Span, The Washington Post and the Korea Today Newspaper (Seoul, South Korea).

Mark has shared the stage with former U.S. Attorney General Janet Reno, Senator John McCain, Magic Johnson, Edward James Olmos, Grammy Award winning artists Rihanna, Brooks and Dunn and Brandy, Academy Award nominated actor Liam Neeson, CEO Bob Nardelli (Home Depot), Steve Case (AOL/Time Warner), Ken Thompson (Wachovia), Jeff Swartz (Timberland) and Ben and Jerry (Ben and Jerry's Ice Cream).

Throughout his entertainment career, Mark has performed for the Tuskegee Airmen, the Secretary of the Interior Gayle Norton, Secretary of Commerce Don Evans, Secretary of Labor Elaine Chao, Members of Congress, Sargent Shriver, Mia Hamm, Tony Stewart,

The Washington Redskins, The Atlanta Falcons, and The New York Giants (NFL), the Florida Panthers (NHL), the Washington Nationals (MLB), the NCAA, Universal Studios and The Supreme Allied Commander of NATO Europe.

Currently, Mark travels the country delivering keynote addresses for businesses, colleges, young professionals networks, conferences and school assemblies. He also performs the National Anthem for collegiate and professional sports teams and is the full-time National Anthem singer for the University of North Dakota Men's Hockey program as well as a guest performer for the College World Series, WE Fest, The Minnesota Twins and the Los Angeles Dodgers.

Mark co-founded Breath Is Limited Motivational Speaking and Entertainment, LLC in order to advance ideas and ignite passion all over the world. Information on his company can be found at www.BreathIsLimited.com

Mark is a former Sergeant in the United States Air Force and an Afghanistan War Veteran who currently lives in Fargo, North Dakota.Mark currently lives in Fargo, North Dakota.

Mark J. Lindquist

Jared L. Bye

About the Co-Author Jared L. Bye

Jared L. Bye is a serial entrepreneur who currently owns, controls and manages Breath is Limited Motivational Speaking and Entertainment. He is also the owner of a financial planning firm based out of Fargo, North Dakota and a sales and marketing consulting firm with a client base throughout the eastern United States.

In his role at Breath is Limited Motivational Speaking and Entertainment, Jared represents clients throughout the United States. He consults with speakers and entertainers, negotiates contracts on the client's behalf and books gigs for the speaker/entertainer after a brief trial period. Jared works with speakers who are brand new to the business as well as seasoned veterans of the stage. No matter the level of experience, Jared's managerial expertise has proven to be an invaluable component of a performer's success.

As Mark J. Lindquist's business manager, Jared is the co-author of this book. He is also the marketing consultant and lead speechwriter who co-wrote two of Mark's TED Talks. Together, Jared and Mark will share their work with over a half-a-million people in the year 2014.

Contacting Mark, Jared and Breath Is Limited Motivational Speaking and Entertainment:

You can contact the business office at Breath Is Limited Motivational Speaking and Entertainment, LLC at:

3120-Z 25th Street South
Suite 160
Fargo, ND 58103

You may email us at:
Mark@BreathIsLimited.com
Jared@BreathIsLimited.com

Websites: www.BreathIsLimited.com
                  www.MarkJLindquist.com

Twitter: @MarkJLindquist

Facebook: Mark J. Lindquist

Instagram: MarkJLindquist